TO NANA & POP: GRETA AND FRANK WILKINS;
MOM & DAD: VIRGINIA AND HAROLD HILLERY;
MY WIFE AND CHILDREN: MARY, TONI, ZACHARY, AND RAECHEL HILLERY;
MY RIGHT HAND, VANESSA VINCENT; ABBE LENTZ, FOR HER HELP WRITING THIS;
THE HARDWORKING STAFF OF HARLEM GROWN;
AND THE ORIGINAL HARLEM GROWN CHILDREN: NEVAEH, EPIPHANY, KADIATU,
GORGUI, AISSATOU, AND NANTEEN; AND ALL THE
WONDERFUL KIDS OF HARLEM WHO MAKE OUR WORK SO SPECIAL.—T. H.

IN MEMORY OF MY FATHER, ROBERT E. HARTLAND.
RAISED IN A GARDENLESS APARTMENT IN BROOKLYN, NEW YORK,
AND THE SON OF IRISH IMMIGRANTS, HE WENT ON TO BLISSFULLY
GROW ROSES, DOGWOOD, HYDRANGEAS, AND DAHLIAS IN HIS
SUBURBAN WASHINGTON, D.C., YARD.—J. H.

The author's portion of proceeds from this book are being paid directly to Harlem Grown, Inc. For more information about Harlem Grown, please visit harlemgrown.org.

SIMON & SCHUSTER BOOKS FOR YOUNG READERS · An imprint of Simon & Schuster Children's Publishing Division · 1230 Avenue of the Americas, New York, New York 10020 · Author's note copyright © 2020 by Harlem Grown, Inc. · Text copyright © 2020 by Simon & Schuster, Inc. · Illustrations copyright © 2020 by Jessie Hartland · All rights reserved, including the right of reproduction in whole or in part in any form. · SIMON & SCHUSTER BOOKS FOR YOUNG READERS is a trademark of Simon & Schuster, Inc. · For information about special discounts for bulk purchases, please contact Simon & Schuster Special Sales at 1-866-506-1949 or business@simonandschuster.com. · The Simon & Schuster Speakers Bureau can bring authors to your live event. For more information or to book an event, contact the Simon & Schuster Speakers Bureau at 1-866-248-3049 or visit our website at www.simonspeakers.com. · Book design by Lucy Ruth Cummins · The text for this book was set in Blocky Fill. · The illustrations for this book were rendered in gouache. · Manufactured in China · 1221 SCP 10 9 8 7 · Library of Congress Cataloging-in-Publication Data · Names: Hillery, Tony, author. | Hartland, Jessie, illustrator. · Title: Harlem Grown : how one big idea transformed a neighborhood / Tony Hillery ; illustrated by Jessie Hartland. · Description: First edition. | New York : A Paula Wiseman Book, Simon & Schuster Books for Young Readers, [2020] | Includes bibliographical references. | Audience: Ages 4–8 | Audience: Grades 2-3 | Summary: "Once there was a lot full of trash. Now there is a lush, green farm. This is the story of Harlem Grown, a garden in New York City"—Provided by publisher. Identifiers: LCCN 2019028125 (print) | LCCN 2019028126 (eBook) | ISBN 9781534402317 (hardback) | ISBN 9781534402324 (eBook) · Subjects: LCSH: Urban agriculture—New York—Juvenile literature. | Community gardens—New York—Juvenile literature. · Classification: LCC S451.N56 H55 2020 (print) | LCC S451.N56 (eBook) | DDC 635.9/77—dc23 · LC record available at https://lccn.loc.gov/2019028125 · LC eBook record available at https://lccn.loc.gov/2019028126

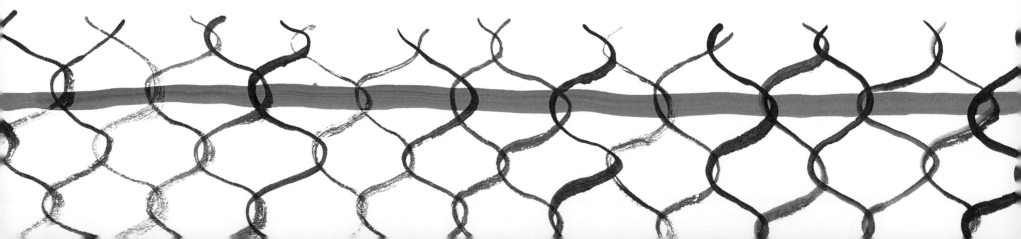

HOW ONE BIG IDEA TRANSFORMED A NEIGHBORHOOD

HARLEM GROWN

WRITTEN BY TONY HILLERY

ILLUSTRATED BY JESSIE HARTLAND

A Paula Wiseman Book · Simon & Schuster Books for Young Readers

New York London Toronto Sydney New Delhi

Once,
in a big city
called New York,
in a bustling
neighborhood
called Harlem,

there was
an empty lot.

Nevaeh called it the haunted garden.
It was cluttered with wrecked couches,
old TVs, broken bottles, and empty cans.

Once,
in a big city,
in a bustling
neighborhood,
there was Nevaeh's school.

PS 175 it was called, and it sat across
from the haunted garden.

One day a man came to PS 175. Mr. Tony, the kids called him.

When Mr. Tony saw
those kids and
that haunted garden,
he had an idea.

He began to clear
the haunted garden,

one piece of trash
at a time.

Soon it was a clean slate.

A blank canvas.

Mr. Tony laid down new, clean soil.

He invited
Nevaeh
to help.

pure

Fertilizer

organic

50 POUNDS

seeds

RADISH

CARROT

seeds

seeds

BASIL

SEEDS

Tomato

CATNIP

SEEDS

Parsley

SEEDS

Seeds.

Shovels.

* PINE BARK *

mulch

50 POUNDS

Seeds

MINT

organic

TOPSOIL

PURE + rich   50 lbs.

Water.

Nevaeh started to plant.

Then she dug holes
in the ground.

Into the holes,
she placed her seedlings,
and then she carefully
covered them with dirt.

Her friends
came too.

Four hundred seedlings went into the ground, one for each kid.

Basil,

mint,

cilantro,

rosemary.

Then the kids
watered

and weeded,

and their plants

began to grow.

Once when Nevaeh came
to the lot after school,
her plant was wilted and sad.

"We'll try again," said Mr. Tony. "We'll plant something different."

Wood.
Hammer.
Nails.

Mr. Tony built raised beds for the plants.

The kids tried again.

and broccoli,

Peas

eggplants.

mint and

PEAS

Broccoli

MINT

EGGPLANT

FULL SUN

ORGANIC

peppermint

Acme SEED Co.

They watered and weeded,

and at last . . .

tomatoes, cucumbers, peppers, blueberries, strawberries, collard greens, kale, basil, arugula.

Mr. Tony watched and helped and smiled.
More kids came from the neighborhood.

They tended their plants, which grew and grew.
Up came more fruits and vegetables.

The kids took their green beans and carrots and cucumbers home to their families for dinner.

Once,
in a big
city called
New York,

HARLEM
GROWN
GARDEN

in a bustling neighborhood called Harlem,
there was a man with an idea.

There were kids who wanted to help.
And they made a farm.

DEAR READER,

First things first. There's something I want you all to know. I am no garden expert. I'll even let you in on a secret: I have killed more plants than I have been able to grow! I knew nothing about what it takes to grow a single plant, let alone start an entire farm, but I saw a problem that I wanted to fix.

In 2010 I closed my company when the economy took a turn. I began to volunteer at PS 175 in Harlem. Like many in Harlem, the underfunded school had no art or gym classes. At lunchtime the students had so much pent-up energy that they would often find themselves in trouble. The blocks around PS 175 are host to fifty-five fast food restaurants and twenty-nine pharmacies, but not a single store from which to purchase healthy food. When I noticed the vacant lot across from the school, I had the idea to begin Harlem Grown.

Now the kids and their parents, with the support of the Harlem Grown staff, grow thousands of pounds of fruits and vegetables a year, which they give to their neighbors and community—free of charge. After school and on weekends, local kids flock to the garden to tend their vegetables and fruits. Incidents in the cafeteria decreased dramatically because the farm encourages collaboration and patience. I realized that many of these students growing up in the concrete jungle didn't know where a tomato came from until they were introduced to Harlem Grown's farms. Now, they happily eat fresh vegetables because they're proud to have grown them themselves.

Originally one garden plot on 134th Street, our urban farm has expanded to twelve sites across Harlem.

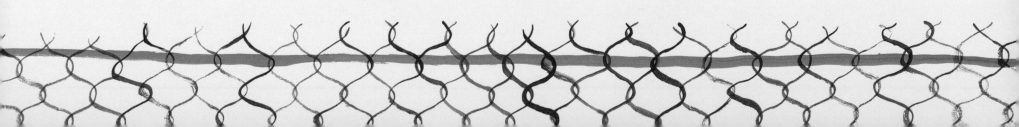

It employs twenty-two full-time staff members, who provide administrative support, additional crop mainte-nance, and go into schools to teach nutrition and sustainability, and most importantly, mentor children daily. At Harlem Grown, the mentors are all young men and women from the community, and they work hard to teach and inspire the kids about healthy eating while also studying hard to complete their education.

The little patch where it all began still exists, and every summer the sweetest strawberries in all of New York City grow and are eaten by the children who tend to their urban farm.

**SINCERELY,
TONY HILLERY**
Founder and Director
of Harlem Grown

START A GARDEN ANYWHERE

STEP 1:

Find a place to begin your garden. A plant needs four things to grow: sun, soil, water, and air. Make sure your growing space gets sunlight at some point during the day. Make sure the area isn't cluttered, so there can be plenty of air flow. Make sure your plants are in a place where you can water them daily. No space is too small—a windowsill, a backyard patio, an empty corner of a schoolyard.

STEP 2:

Plants will grow in any container. Collect large pots, milk crates, even old car tires. Get some soil from your local hardware store. Fill your containers with soil. If you can, make your own compost from your kitchen scraps and add that to the soil.

STEP 3:

Get some seeds from the hardware store. Get seeds for your favorite vegetable. Get seeds for something you've never tried eating before. Using your hands, plant the seeds in your pots, containers, or beds (raised wooden frames with soil in them), making sure to do so with special care. Most seed packets have all the information you need to know for planting the seeds.

STEP 4:

Take every chance you can to learn more about your garden. Seek the knowledge of others. The best gardens are the ones that have been influenced by many people. Go to your local library, go look at different community and school gardens, talk about your garden with everybody. You never know who has a unique take on gardening.

STEP 5:

Tend to your plants daily by watering, weeding, and pruning. Pay close attention: check the leaves and the quality of the soil, and keep an eye out for pests, like aphids or hornworms. Catching pests early will help you save your garden! Gardening is a constant learning process. Every week you will see changes and understand your garden in a different way.

STEP 6:

When your plants are ready to harvest, invite friends, family, and neighbors to cook and eat together!

ADDITIONAL RESOURCES

For all ages:

Web

harlemgrown.org

jmgkids.us/kids-zone/jmgkidsweb

kidsgardening.org/gardening-basics

extension.illinois.edu/firstgarden/basics

Books

Gibbons, Gail. *From Seed to Plant*. New York: Holiday House, 1991.

Gibbons, Gail. *The Vegetables We Eat*. New York: Holiday House, 2007.

Krezel, Cindy. *Kids' Container Gardening: Year-Round Projects for Inside and Out*. Chicago: Chicago Review Press, 2010.

Lerner, Carol. *My Backyard Garden*. New York: William Morrow & Co., 1998.

Tornio, Stacy. *Project Garden: A Month-By-Month Guide to Planting, Growing, and Enjoying ALL Your Backyard Has to Offer*. Avon, MA: Adams Media, 2012.

For adults:

Web

For an extensive list of resources about starting a community or school garden, visit

n2ncentre.com/education-support/parent-resources/

For information about starting a school garden, visit

slowfoodusa.org/resources-and-grants

brightbites.ca/wp-content/uploads/seeds-for-success-final.pdf

For information about starting a garden in containers in your home or school, visit

eatright.org

Books

Bucklin-Sporer, Arden, and Rachel Kathleen Pringle. *How to Grow a School Garden: A Complete Guide for Parents and Teachers*. Portland, OR: Timber Press, 2010.

Carpenter, Novella, and Willow Rosenthal. *The Essential Urban Farmer*. New York: Penguin Books, 2011.